field guide to autobiography

MELISSA ELEFTHERION

-- the operating system c. 2018 --

the operating system
print//document

FIELD GUIDE TO AUTOBIOGRAPHY

ISBN: 978-1-946031-37-2
Library of Congress Control Number: 2018939195

edited and designed by Lynne DeSilva-Johnson
with assistant copyediting by Jacq Greyja and Erick Sáenz

This text was set in Steelworks Vintage, The Constellation of Heracles, Minion, and OCR-A Standard, printed and bound by Spencer Printing, in Honesdale, PA, in the USA. Books from The Operating System are distributed to the trade by SPD/Small Press Distribution, with ePub and POD via Ingram.

Note: an earlier version of this text appeared in publication in 2017,
by the no longer operating H_NGM_N EDITIONS.

The operating system is a member of the Radical Open Access Collective, a community of scholar-led, not-for-profit presses, journals and other open access projects. Now consisting of 40 members, we promote a progressive vision for open publishing in the humanities and social sciences. Learn more at: http://radicaloa.disruptivemedia.org.uk/about/

the operating system
141 Spencer Street #203
Brooklyn, NY 11205
www.theoperatingsystem.org
operator@theoperatingsystem.org

— —field guide to autobiography — —

MELISSA ELEFTHERION

AUTO/

\BIO

FIELD GRAPH [NO GUIDE]/

AUTO/

i made myself from rocks
shells   birds   insects   trees
mountain   and   ocean
i made myself   as you have   carapace
this is an autobiography of fractures
this is a field guide to a field guide
to identity   that muscular slap of light

A human is a half-way house to a bird
Whiplike flagella that lash back and forth
Poking at echinodermata, appropriating invertebrate
          wraith

Is I what it means to be a self
A stomach the length of a performer's discretion
Granularity of its stain—a tree ring

All night the hard fatty substance applied,
Slurps with an enlarged pink.
What are the attempted catechisms masochisms
The wind a push of carnivorous ghosts

terns

A small, feathered race

Underparts   may   be

mostly insects

Distinguished from familiar face patterns

The family
mandible   The highly pelagic

Distinguished is the only other

A low-pitched snapping head

A w a k e in the coverts   Awake
under the common
fur

Distinctive over the water

cormorants

unwary green it calls

out

hairy breasted feathered advances

developing in
the scolding rattle

developing under the hot
fluorescents

a throat exposed a thorax
mined

immature in
the white its larvae a blister reaching upward

a small soaring singly

winged, stalked.

Common, common, uncommon
Distinguished from other wrens
Distinguished from the loon

The daily biology of the yield
Grey matter on a micro slide
Rub hind legs against

Females of a few species produce soft noises
Both pairs of wings sometimes small or absent
Note the inconspicuous jerking of its long tail

The song higher
Feeding mainly on bright buffy underparts
Feeding mainly with bright scolding rattles

Wings stalked at base
Washed off abdomen
Spend an ocean attached

The carapace of haunt
A sound-producing apparatus
Restless, resemble, raptorial hind feet
Archery of a heart plucked back—
its steel reverb, Listen.

Phosphorescent composition
Under-glass -   prisms
a gem stone   instrument

Areas of tissue
Shaped like a first-born child
The nucleus in animal salts
The splitting of the crown

A kind of gelatin
Plastic coating a religious discourse
Plastic coating the waterfall
A protective film

Granular circles in circles
Her metic index
Ain't got a skeletal

abalone

aperture   a nacre of unraveling

for man-made food or jewelry   a stained rainbow

iridescent rib   a flesh shell takes with air

variable openings

feathered in the rough   a scaly convex

the shiny inside breathes   a pulsing shimmer

lust disguised as dreaming

orthoptera

predaceous calling song
gets the sexes

together hairlike
feeders

distance a mouth in the long-horned basement

hind legs call immature rubbing

body party

metamorphosis simple

the apple tree

gnarled & picturesque

curling, their wounds

wrap around

each other for comfort

vigilance veined bark a soft
gray

in the s t a r r e d c h a m b e r

toothed edges

a flourish of rust and scabs

the paper birch

skin in the pale sheets

young a yellow brown tinged red

crunching through

the soft memory of tomorrow

w e
peeled

it back

family

etched years into your oblique

we were reeds then
SWALLOWS

sky

leaves

a milk

of galloping ghost

Rattle, esophagus waist. Dewlap, forelimb. Popliteal
fossa.
Eggtooth, climb cloaca. Anterior astrogalus.
Keel, brain, keel. Hoof, patella. Auditory meatus.
Wishbone tail feather. Vibrissa.
(bile duct)
Lumbar, carapace.   Incisor shell.
((buccal cavity))
Cardiac orifice.

acolyte elytra
occipital petal
fecal parietal cloacal

pull the lever peevish scullion
that's right keep pulling
    parhelion

erasiromotor

Ambulatory intense discard
as if with branches, drawn axes
To scale erosion with wall figures held to a fire
To become solemnly visible, gratification of the body
A curving, a fabric, tidal device a study of
Subatomic music the absolute brightness

At the junction of two substances exposed to light—
a high altitude baby, a mouth

They have a rubbery delirium Living colorless relating
A subdivision established for politics
Fixed aquatic invertebrates

To grow into a tree A graceful, dry flammable leap.
And yet we place all our messy in moments of looking

Obsolete inventories The tide of the denuded
We were using music.

flycatchers

buffy buffy wingbars

of immature

the call

common common a
commons

the distinctive
between

little or no

in spruce fir

in wood margins

impossible to identify

Usually lamellate, sometimes flabellate.[1]
Call is an ascending whistle.[2]
Tegulae present. Body flattened.[3]
Deciduous, show enough face pattern to separate.[4]
All killing jars should be wiped out occasionally.
Wingbeats slow enough to be counted.

----

[1] (superfamily scarabaeid)
[2] (common loon)
[3] (achilid planthopper)
[4] (bridled titmouse)

shell wing. chrysalis leaf sun. apex alula.
                    head blade corona.
whorl, great coverts. mesothorax. cuticle gas.
spires primaries. wing. petiole. radioactive
suture mirror. segment midrib.
               ____________ labrum.
______ antenna sheath.photosphere.
siphonal tertial. cremaster stipule. core.

digitized domain

This skeleton of tiny needles This object in an electrical field
Persons or the general plastic
The process of photographing digital objects

A film of extravascular Originating in igneous an appendage
Shaped by worry stones Rebellion marked with liner

Any of several shrub species point to their horns
Lend plasma to the earliest silicate

The conversion of gratuitous benefit
Another term includes relatives

See them water the girl watching sparks

bioluminadolescence

When light sticks inside bodies
The viscous imaginary
A protective sheath, a plastic coating, a waterfall

Orbital schema – an awkward grinding
Grey over buoyant grey, a rainbow scrape

When light sticks inside bodies
Bug jelly maths
Porifera make new hydras
Give Zeus the finger

A parthenogenetic hum
Stuns the ocean floor

Leaves shoot duodenal refuse
A vein of cellular debris
But, to chop it—
A clutch of pearls through the stained glass
A pawing at the branches

When light is a family of bones
When light deviates

the specimen

Mesothorax—Large energy heart field
At the attachment Swollen segments
A yellow sun, a black sun Between the wings yellow

The length of imago Dorsal longitude
Denticulated at basal half
A nymph's inconvenience A collection of pet insects
Specimen—Generally speaking, among the tentacles

Fossilized species The contents are granular
Changes of skin occur The larvae, the pupae, lacunae
Thoracic atmosphere
The insect is exhausted Weak and feeble light, wings glissant

catalpa

tiny glands   of heart leaf

the inside of a blossom
radial star a first from the bottom a fist
flowers a radiolaria a burst a bloom

lilac   white & a yellow

the thing

that used
to   hit   me

heavy frost   makes for thicker bark

the tree her bruised shadow made

a slightly hairy green

elytra meat

That little girl already a slut to you on roller-skates.
Elytra truncate and not much taller than wide.

Hand job in the schoolyard.
Arista rises at base of 3rd antennal segment.

Asphalt peeled off her like skin.
Occurs at fresh sap flows on trees.

Good attendance reward.
Larvae can jump.

Bra straps showing.
Does not reach tegula.

Meat on the shelf.
Mouthparts chewing

katydids

in high pitched lisps or ticks

sings only at night

dorsal

arboreal

in the trees

of the trees

fine hairs

horizontal
slender
antennae

katy-did katy-didn't

/BIO

snails

to   breathe   is   to   go
inside

eye of my tentacle

no shells   no shells at all

Organism disreputable open sloth
a circular prison arranged with scales
waste matter separated, a hard pale green
hot, hot dust denoting glands
fatty larvae relating at the funeral.

Comestible a volatile fluid Southern
the large bulbs of which a formal
authorization showy red or yellow
flowers a star after the first
it came to me in flesh

In the slick of the gradual lack
The more viscous, the barrier.
A river, and mingled with her
A fertile containing.
More specifically, shape derived.
Parallel the faces of familiar
A smokeless explosive,
A lively secretion dance.

O Larvae, I never meant you harm.

sea cucumber

spines buried deep
tentacles grown over and again
a skeleton mouth
to grab the crumbs
to be inside a body
there is a fur

Spinneret, lining up the beams,
"Get outta here, I already own this leaf"
The energy gained,
A lot of work before collisions,
Dragging coccygeal around the dirt lot,
Balloons tied to a shopping cart,
Birds crossing intersections.

wrens

loud bubbling song

laid in the
cavities

common common uncommon

familiar migrant
an identity insect

it may even sing
lack of a dark

unmusical trills

a nest a familiar
a clear-eyed rattle

bright buffy underparts a bell

low-pitched in the sedge

boobys

immature a rare visitor a swoop and tucks

family a
long line
of robbers
g e n t l e
gliders

all the flight feathers

dark underparts

all warm oceans

stoneflies (plecoptera)

soft-bodied for stone

leaves
wing margin
of water

poor fliers underdeveloped mandibles

diurnal nocturnal
diurnal

in algae

no remnants of nymphal gills ghosts

predaceous the soft
rest

sexually active [first speculum]

Working girls get the butter
An inedible sea wall
Echolocates the rasp
Of insect ecology
A clasp of the spiny-legged
Mouths multitask
The ultrasound
A beam of genital strategies

a mollusk heliopause

in cerebral tentacle

pore bubble interstellar

winking her copulatory
bursa

she bow pedal particles

statocyst
gone with eyes

no gills

in a bump her gas magnet a sheath

amygdala basal

tail
numb with
hydrogen
shock

accelerated ganglion

genital
pleural

stomach the galaxy shell between

scarab beetles (coleoptera)

heavy-bodied oval

laid egg

digs a
hole

margins of the elytra

head in a ball
hind legs close together

damage done by larvae or adults

dilated and spiny

feeds on foliage fruits flowers

feeds under the bark in juices

my aborted fetus visits coney island circus sideshow

The eggs are laid in the galleries
We wander, plucking faces from white walls
The yolk demands its attachment
The yolk broadcasts the feed

A nest of small beaks, a nest of plumes
In circles, circles
Wingless, a shiny cadence
Tufted f-stop heart
Lets light in, brave

The fight is feathery distance but we claw its shimmer of idea
A hologram that pops up strata with puffed chins and chest
The shooting gallery where we fire and fire
A high squealing wah wah wah

wilderness meat a feathered breathing

a many-skinned government.   curators of the unctuous.
the plaintive with welts. we are alarming, cheerful. any of
various meats. sensitive to high winds.

developed in the ghost of natural light.   we climb
the glowing clock.
wound of my habit. perpendicular to mature wins.   a fur
of families.

any of various. time the clematis.   up up the young or
eggs. someday to uncoiling.

breathing in feathers.   the regularly occurring
copulation.   large, non-

migratory.   and stridulating.   rubbing my
species

an underground rhizome of chirping, abolishing

play back the offensive flattering
play back the wilderness

any old-world tropical iconoclast   any of several
grasses for the overthrow

the numerous, the diptera
larvae in wounds

ossuary with a wide spout //   self-feeding in the
sea green.

a genus changed into a spring //   a genus mundane in the
latitudes.

we built this self on the sea

to curate a chapel we put our hands together and blew
in warmer latitudes a glimpse of ocean mouth
the sea-green beyond finger steeple

a self of units
song a decorated structure
any starling
any rattle

we migrate from saltwater
any of creeping various
the body of the lower
amatory, saclike
family of egress

annelid

a life in circles
inner lip of a mollusk
annelid the conch of my
melting shape

barnacle larvae
comb bearer a spiny skin
inner mandala a lotus flame
the center is mercy

i give birth to myself

Historicity changes

in the water body

The aurora call

The line in pieces

Gaps in the static

Botanica a hermetic

neutrino

Aurora born of glass

subatombotanies

I was a piece of quilted lace edible seaweed a small cavity
an order of crustaceans I refused the mouth refused the
mannered baby refused seven similar pairs of legs

Of, relating to or being subatomic witchcraft their tissues
in high frequency Their products denote glands secrete in
vestibules directly source electron surgery

A contradiction an algebraic hand-job medicine for the
small areas An error with a cutaway Irregular patches of
shavings Rubber thrown in a scalene game

A bee flown in the mouth *A single opening ringed with*
tentacles   Rust and salt

Horizontal and non-linear a distant cup-shaped body
A mass of tree shells   revealed   in distant eyes

The shell overlaps tectonic shifts I hydrate the empire
Wasted botanies long latitudes developed separately
Taxonomic babies in dust wiped their edges to fit neatly
Capable   poised   on the base of a leaf

In its daughter cells a rattle acapella All delirium of
decrees and doctrines   fallen ridiculed   phylum
Its bark and bone in the gristle of embrace
Rolled up like a thick cuticle

pink milkweed

the leaves are opposite

composition boiled in several changes of water

in angles

only slightly spreading
only slightly species

plant parts
to make sticky
like ordinary milk

coarse
&
climbing

rhodochrosite

brittle   *cleavage*

veined light

beading

metastasis

a pearlescent gravity

a conch in the milky   dissolves

granule by granule

the crystals on weathering

abalone

the muscle of metamorphosis

a vigorous tiny shell

in rainbow margins eaten and eaten

in the hatches

blister pearls

to my grandmother—devout, flawed simple grit
the button jar was opportunity

nacreous rib for whirligigs
all iridescence greasy

opal

a play of rainbow glass
amorphous, hardened deposits
a pseudopath

collected for its fluorescence
the cells magnify when perturbed

the gaps a play on desire
lustre of fragments
a sky made of shards

the flame
higher and higher
insoluble

capitalism's echolocation

i shall burn the fat thigh-bones
larvae feed on dried materials
the act of emancipation
tiny flowers under a microscope

i confess
all stages are predaceous
deep in mammal feathers
introduced in wet places

not an algae
but a community of animals
use your soft hands
the ferocious few or no scales on wings

i have taken off my skirt
a surgical colony
alphabetical assembly

at night in grassy places
a warren of robots
ducking in the hairs of copulation

astartes

the softest parts the brightest

in cold species
shell pieces   margins

combat & halt

truncation of sea starts

washed to the basins

intertidal
          the waves lap up & up

chambered nautilus ii

i will live in the far room
collect my becomings
around me like a hydra
dorsal tetra
head of jurassics

i acquiesce to longing
i will live in shells

mother of the nacreous
of waiting pearls
we are lonesome too
send down your dragons

FIELD GRAPH {NO GUIDE}

tellins

natives of all seas

when home disintegrates
we belong everywhere

specimen rainbow
noble bivalve
come find me

paper nautilus

where the shell escapes
the [sea] [led]
[sea]led off in its float
the sea led the sea
compartmentalized
a flesh filled with puffs of air
where the shell escapes
anteroom   diluvian
mitochondria
little deads little blooms
my crumbling organism

cockle

my heart-shaped secretion
my exposed symmetry
a specimen

in the sediment buried alive

bilateral suction
a siphon

i am edible in shapes

the halides

salt the insides
coax the soluble
"in each cube face"
a desire for desire
the melting of classification
where the white crusts around
where the crystals form
colorless, a conchoidal fracture
repeated or blue among
the gases
this is a group of soft bones breaking
this is a history of capitalism.

the oxides

This is a group
This is a salt
All the cube face formations
All the little depressions in the cubes

Where go the igneous bust
porphyry a molt of milk
in seams
in cuts across the rocks
the ragged interiors of aging

We make room for yellow first
drips of sediment

This is the species
All the gaps are leaking
All the little darks fill the gaps

human > bird < starfish > plant < earthworm

human   bird   starfish   plant   earthworm
skull   crown   ______   terminal bud   _______
eye   eye   sieve plate   _______   _______
mandible.   mandible   beak   _______   roots   mouth cavity
scapula   scapulars   ray   branch   _______
breast   breast   _______   third node   _______
wingspan   wing covert   ray   flower   stalk
heart   heart   cardiac portion   _______   lateral heart
belly   belly   digestive gland   _______   gizzard
anus   rump   anus   stem   dorsal blood vessel
feet   wing   tube feet   tap root   ______________

rocking boat incantation

Tectonic the winds to tuck neatly fur is field;
Hind feathered females hide the sun, yield muscle,
measure larvae the subatomic;

Make mountain a shell of.

Weather determines aperture

The volatile; Deciduous nacreous.

Rubbing chrysalis wiped intersections

predaceous bug oops spines milk.

Why now sea dragons under porphyry and bees a skinned grey gravity

Pull the lever, diatoms

the cuticle begins to open

Skins pull, the field a radiolaria.
Integument

Fluorescent wounds a scab against the pseudopath.

Flammable mouth echolocates the rasp
Fur species   in lust gaps

The crystals were wet skeleton music
Heliopause a magnet for larvae.
The lack.

hydra in her own dust

My own face on the chop places margin.
Concrete starling

Brick thorax
Scales rust the soft galaxy

Shells in coccygeal ocean starts, lisps
Scolding   subcutaneous   birds cavity a rubbing of soft bones.

Scabs carapace   vibrissa meat   capitalism petroleum handjobs
a tiny echinodermata.

A colony of salts   Dust copulatory
Latitudes tissues a hologram

Phylum wing fractures truncation
Jar   Harm   Elytra   (my hand releases)

Legs soft rainbow off glass distinctive;
Cuticle the coated   the underparts   folded   small plastic fire;

Magnetic or crustacean heart;
Metamorphosis I tree.

that time a tree grew out of my mouth & I had armor

auriculars hinge mandible

what is the mouth of a tree ocean

breast a pallial line thorax

my cambium

i am armor in the woods
piths
capito-pedal cartilage

Alula little hinge elytra my growth rings
my tentacles

The orbital in umbo coxa
Undertail coverts ligament

The heart is a phloem
a muscle scar a gut of ganglia

Radula along leaf margins

I graze the little points with my teeth
i draw a line

in the skinned phylum

we're all becoming animals here
our scaly skins showing through the stained glass
why now why slither
the rainbow gate beneath suit sleeves
beneath chiffon and tweed
the rainbow plexus in our throats

once a wren ever an abalone shell
we were whole once
wander detritus wonder
the furs in the soft air
gentle browns of wood and bark
as the furs gallop by

identify me
call me into
curiosity pinwheel
i make little sparks

in recent lavas
we were the hands holding
tectonic/footstep
we were the under
and beneath

to speak in soil tongues
to be called into ditches
to be summoned
venal wing
wet black eros pitch

leaf matter and dirt cake
the cavity I root
small declivities of teeth
along the rim
how the mouth knows

we were once rose quartz
we were agate
smashed and smashed
among the rock
your smooth body a reminder

---source notes---

/AUTO:

the eggs are laid in the galleries... -
The first and last lines are quotations derived from *A field guide to insects: America North of Mexico* (Embioptera order) and *A guide to field identification: Birds of North America* (White-Fronted Goose), respectively.

/BIO:

In composing */bio*, I frequently consulted three texts that found their way into my collection through serendipitous means. All italicized language in */bio* is directly quoted from *A field guide to insects: America North of Mexico, Book of Trees* and *A guide to field identification: Birds of North America.*

Borror, Donald J. & White, Richard E. (Eds.) (1970). *A field guide to insects: America North of Mexico*. New York, NY: Houghton Mifflin.

Mills, Lewis H. & Hawkins, Gertrude C. (Eds.) (1939). *Book of Trees.* Chicago, IL: Rand McNally.

Robbins, Chandler S., Bruun, Bertel, & Zim, Herbert S. (Eds.) (1966). *A guide to field identification: Birds of North America.* New York, NY: Golden Press.

/FIELD GRAPH [NO GUIDE]:

In composing *field graph [no guide]*, I slept with, gleaned, & carried with me two texts that colonized my thought processes & informed my poetry:

Low, Donald. (1961). *The How and Why Wonder Book of Seashells.* New York, NY: Wonder Books.

Pough, Frederick H. (1960). *A Field Guide to Rocks and Minerals.* Cambridge, MA: Houghton Mifflin, The Riverside Press Cambridge.

/ACKNOWLEDGMENTS

Thank you to the editors of the following publications in which poems from field guide to autobiography previously appeared:

Menacing Hedge: “a human is a halfway house”

Truck: “terns,” “wrens,” and “boobys”

Tinderbox Poetry Journal: “cormorants” and “subatombotanies”

Dusie: “erasiromotor,” “digitized domain,” “the specimen,” “winged, stalked,” and “bioluminadolescence”

NICE CAGE: “catalpa”

Open Letters Monthly: “abalone”

Entropy: “the paper birch,” “the apple tree,” “capitalism’s echolocation” as “animal skirt,” “annelid,” “loons,” “chambered nautilus II,” and “sea cucumber”

Letterbox Magazine: “acolyte elytra,” “Rattle, esophagus waist,” and “a mollusk heliopause”

Peacock Online Review : “in the slick of the gradual lack” and “at the junction”

Otoliths: “Elytra Meat”

DUSIE blog: “katydids”

Mom Egg Review: “my aborted fetus visits Coney Island Circus Sideshow” as “mama, turn out the light”

Flag+Void:“the halides” and “the oxides”

Queen Mob’s Teahouse: “wilderness meat a feathered breathing”

Delirious Hem: “opal”

Bone Bouquet: “sexually active [first speculum]” as “clasp”

Negative Capability: “abalone II”

Glass: A Journal of Poetry: “that time a tree grew out of my mouth & i had armor”

INDEX/_LIFE FORMS

eukaryota__

animalia__

animalia_arthropoda_insecta_plecoptera / 44
animalia_euarthropoda_insecta_hymenoptera_bee / 55, 71
animalia_euarthropoda_insecta_coleoptera / 32, 73, 75
animalia_arthropoda_insecta_coleoptera_scarabaeoidea / 47
animalia_chordata_aves_bird / 11, 41, 70, 73
animalia_chordata_aves_charadriiformes_laridae_tern / 12
animalia_chordata_aves_passeriformes_certhioformes_
troglodytidae_wren / 15, 42, 75
animalia_chordata_aves_gaviiformes_gaviidae_loon / 15
animalia_chordata_aves_passeriformes_muscicapidae_flycatcher / 15
animalia_chordata_aves_passeriformes_sturnidae_starling / 73
animalia_chordata_aves_pelecaniformes_phalacrocoracidae_corcomant / 14

plantae__

plantae_angiosperms_eudicots_betulacaea_b. papyrifera (paper birch) / 20
plantae_angiosperms_eudicots_bignoniaceae_catalpa / 31
plantae_angiosperms_malus_m. pumila (apple tree) / 19
plantae_angiosperms_apocynaceae_pink milkweed / 55

minerale__

calcite_magnesium acido aero mineralisatum_rhodochrosite / 56
cristobalite_opal / 58
quartz porphyry_porphyry / 69
chalcedony_agate / 76
quartz_quarzo rosa / 76

GRATITUDES

I am joyfully grateful to friends and teachers who have encouraged and supported my work. Many thanks to Diane di Prima, Elise Ficarra, Bhanu Kapil, and Juliana Spahr for their brave teachings and radical understanding. Thank you to Michalle Gould for early, close readings of this work. Thank you so much to the indefatigable Lynne DeSilva-Johnson & The OS for uplifting and believing in this work—your support has meant everything. Many thanks to my mom, Marie Sitaro for being fearless & bold. Special thanks to my family: Kevin & Phoenix Carr—I learn from you both everyday.

MELISSA ELEFTHERION grew up in Brooklyn. A high school dropout, she went on to earn an MFA in Poetry from Mills College and an MLIS from San Jose State University. She is the author of *huminsect, prism maps, Pigtail Duty, the leaves the leaves, green glass asterisms, little ditch*, and several other chapbooks. Founder of the Poetry Center Chapbook Exchange, Melissa lives in Northern California where she works as a Reference & Teen Services Librarian, teaches creative writing, & curates the LOBA Reading Series at the Ukiah Library. *field guide to autobiography* is her first full-length collection.

POETICS AND PROCESS: A CONVERSATION

with melissa eleftherion
& lynne desilva-johnson

Greetings comrade!
Thank you for talking to us about your process today!
Can you introduce yourself, in a way that you would choose?

Hi there! I'm Melissa, a writer/librarian/visual artist person.

Why are you a poet/writer/artist?

So many reasons come to mind, my mental health being primary. I feel more engaged & most alive when I'm writing. It's kept me relatively sane, & isn't something I can easily give up.

When did you decide you were a poet/writer/artist (and/or: do you feel comfortable calling yourself a poet/writer/artist, what other titles or affiliations do you prefer/feel
are more accurate)?

I was seventeen when I committed myself fully to poetry. It was the middle of the night - I was bereft & scared. My brother had come down with a mysterious illness that prompted my mother to take him to the hospital, and I was home to care for my other sibling. I turned to my notebook again for the first time in 4 years, and have been writing myself out of jams since.

Around age 28 when I began studying privately with Diane di Prima & received some validation/motivation to continue, I became more comfortable privately referring to myself as a poet, but bristled at the sound of the word "poet". There's still so much to destigmatize in mainstream culture about what a poet is and does, & it took me a long time to shift my thinking about what the word encapsulates.

What's a "poet" (or "writer" or "artist") anyway?

One who seeks to make things better through poetry and writing and art. One who records failures and triumphs in an attempt towards becoming. One who learns how to translate for a reader/viewer what exists in the mind and heart of both the self and the world. One who is compelled to solve problems and experience sorrows and joys through art-making.

What do you see as your cultural and social role (in the literary / artistic / creative community and beyond)?

As a librarian and an educator, I see myself working to destigmatize poetry & expanding consciousness about what poetry is & is capable of, particularly for youth in my small-town rural community. I incorporate poetry and poetics into as many programs as possible, and work to engage teens with different poetry practices and methods to help them develop ways to use poetry as a tool for their own self-discovery and growth. I also work as a guest poetry instructor at a local high school where I teach various experimental methods and practices to help the teens gain some insight about the expansiveness of poetry as an art form.

As an archivist, I am engaged with the idea of community curation of the continuous present - something Elise Ficarra and I explore a bit with the Poetry Center Chapbook Exchange (PCCE www.poetrychapbooks.omeka.net) The PCCE is a community-curated archive I created and developed for poets to convene, correspond, and collaborate via the currency of the poetry community: chapbooks. In archives, there's this question of who gets to decide what gets saved? Who are the few elite, privileged voices that determine what constitutes our cultural memory and heritage? With the PCCE, one of my goals was to create a participatory archives as a means for poets to both generate work & build towards this cultural memory document together.

Talk about the process or instinct to move these poems (or your work in general) as independent entities into a body of work. How and why did this happen? Have you had this intention for a while? What encouraged and/or confounded this (or a book, in general) coming together? Was it a struggle?

It was a series of accretions and deletions over a span of eight years. The earliest poems were written while I was finishing my degree at Mills, & became part of my MFA thesis in 2007. Participating in NaPoWriMo in April 2014 allowed me to carve out a space to write many of the poems that would later wind up in *field guide to autobiography.*

That April, I had written enough that I could began to see a series emerge and possibly a book. With field guide, once I started seeing where things were going, I began to see connections forming between and among the different genera I was reading about in the various field guides I consulted as source texts. I noticed where the characteristics began to coalesce and formed a semblance of self. That was one of the initial writing processes for the book. I like to let the work tell me where it is going, and try to really tune in and absorb what the poem is about and what it's becoming.

Did you envision this collection as a collection or understand your process as writing or making specifically around a theme while the poems themselves were being written / the work was being made? How or how not?

Yes, though the theme shifted over time. Using field guides as source texts helped me determine the focus for this collection.

What formal structures or other constrictive practices (if any) do you use in the creation of your work? Have certain teachers or instructive environments, or readings/writings/work of other creative people informed the way you work/write?

There are a myriad of formal structures I've employed in my work - erasures, sonnets, chance operations using the *I Ching*, tarot, cut-ups, numerical arrangements. For many years, I've incorporated found language from my autobiographical dictionaries, a series of source texts I've compiled of words new to me discovered through reading.

Studying with Diane di Prima & working as a student-teacher through Poetry for the People helped shape some of my early work which was raw & confessional. Both Juliana Spahr & Will Alexander (along with their work) have had a profound impact on my writing. I've also been influenced by Stephen Ratcliffe's work & his attempts to convey the changes experienced by a landscape over time.

Speaking of monikers, what does your title represent? How was it generated? Talk about the way you titled the book, and how your process of naming (individual pieces, sections, etc) influences you and/or colors your work specifically.

The title, *field guide to autobiography*, grew out of the practice I began in 2014 of using field guides as source texts. Previously, it was titled *autobiotionary*, then *auto/bio*, and finally its current title. *Autobiotionary* was titled for the practice of incorporating found language from the definitions in my autobiographical dictionaries, and questioned the problem of constructing identity around knowledge or ignorance.

With *field guide*, I wanted to explore the inter-relatedness of various species and in so doing, tell a story about the larger body of which they are fragments. Autobiographies are rife with fractures and missing pieces - fragments as form, then. How to describe, comprise, define a life? How does a person begin to enumerate the many fragments & fractals & do they represent a wholeness? The title began as a means of telling the story of various species, and became a field guide to understanding the self through this lens.

What does this particular work represent to you
...as indicative of your method/creative practice?
...as indicative of your history?
...as indicative of your mission/intentions/hopes/plans?

I've had this intuition that we're all fragments of one magnificent, multi-cellular organism and that was the impetus for this book, which I started writing back in 2007 when I was pregnant with my son. While the book has changed dramatically since then, writing into this spatial continuum has compelled me to continue.

Its fulcrum is the teen girls' search for identity in other bodies such as the katydid, the chambered nautilus, & trees. As a teen, I sought refuge in the woods - trees became home to my unraveling &

working through various traumas. I'm also writing from a space of being displaced from one's body, from disassociation as after-effect of sexual abuse and assault. field guide is an attempt at reckoning through the lens of various animals & minerals including katydids, wrens, abalone shells, and apple trees.

What does this book DO (as much as what it says or contains)?

I like to think there's a musicality inherent in the sounding of these organisms throughout the book, and over time they form a song.

What would be the best possible outcome for this book? What might it do in the world, and how will its presence as an object facilitate your creative role in your community and beyond? What are your hopes for this book, and for your practice?

The best possible outcome for this book is that people will read it, and possibly shift their thinking about the need for dominance in ecology to a non-hierarchical, participatory relationship. So yeah, basically - I want to dismantle the patriarchy. In writing field guide, I became more aware of the insidious depths of patriarchal culture & how our many ecosystems are suffused with it.

The presence of this book as an object will facilitate more opportunities to teach experimental writing workshops based on the procedures I used to write it. My hopes are for this book to gain many readers, and to find the stamina & energy to return to working on my latest project, little ditch, a book about being sexualized as a young, non-binary person growing up in rape culture.

Let's talk a little bit about the role of poetics and creative community in social activism, in particular in what I call "Civil Rights 2.0," which has remained immediately present all around us in the time leading up to this series' publication. I'd be curious to hear some thoughts on the challenges we face in speaking and publishing across lines of race, age, privilege, social/cultural background, and sexuality within the community, vs. the dangers of remaining and producing in isolated "silos."

This is a critical time for poetics and creative communities to share resources and support one another against these myriad, heinous assaults on our human rights. There is such strength and resilience and courage in using art to overcome adversity, to educate, to connect, to galvanize, to transform, to activate people to see beyond & keep fighting & caring for themselves and one another. As poets, we have the capacity for shaping language to create new paradigms where racial & cultural differences are celebrated, consent is actively taught to all genders, privilege is acknowledged, and intergenerational communities live among one another symbiotically. Art & language can mobilize people to reshape not only our understanding of ourselves, but also transform our impact as a species.

WHY PRINT/DOCUMENT?

*The Operating System uses the language "print document" to differentiate from the book-object as part of our mission to distinguish the act of documentation-in-book-FORM from the act of publishing as a backwards-facing replication of the book's agentive *role* as it may have appeared the last several centuries of its history. Ultimately, I approach the book as TECHNOLOGY: one of a variety of printed documents (in this case,* bound*) that humans have invented and in turn used to archive and disseminate ideas, beliefs, stories, and other evidence of production.*

Ownership and use of printing presses and access to (or restriction of printed materials) has long been a site of struggle, related in many ways to revolutionary activity and the fight for civil rights and free speech all over the world. While (in many countries) the contemporary quotidian landscape has indeed drastically shifted in its access to platforms for sharing information and in the widespread ability to "publish" digitally, even with extremely limited resources, the importance of publication on physical media has not diminished. In fact, this may be the most critical time in recent history for activist groups, artists, and others to insist upon learning, establishing, and encouraging personal and community documentation practices. Hear me out.

With The OS's print endeavors I wanted to open up a conversation about this: the ultimately radical, transgressive act of creating PRINT /DOCUMENTATION in the digital age. It's a question of the archive, and of history: who gets to tell the story, and what evidence of our life, our behaviors, our experiences are we leaving behind? We can know little to nothing about the future into which we're leaving an unprecedentedly digital document trail — but we can be assured that publications, government agencies, museums, schools, and other institutional powers that be will continue to leave BOTH a digital and print version of their production for the official record. Will we?

As a (rogue) anthropologist and long time academic, I can easily pull up many accounts about how lives, behaviors, experiences — how THE STORY of a time or place — was pieced together using the deep study of correspondence, notebooks, and other physical documents which are no longer the norm in many lives and practices. As we move our creative behaviors towards digital note taking, and even audio and video, what can we predict about future technology that is in any way assuring that our stories will be accurately told - or told at all? How will we leave these things for the record?

In these documents we say:
WE WERE HERE, WE EXISTED, WE HAVE A DIFFERENT STORY

- Lynne DeSilva-Johnson, Founder/Managing Editor,
THE OPERATING SYSTEM, Brooklyn NY 2017

/TITLES IN THE OS PRINT/DOCUMENT SERIES

Śnienie / Dreaming - Marta Zelwan/Krystyna Sakowicz, (Polish-English/dual-language) trans. Victoria Miluch [2019]
Alparegho: Pareil-À-Rien / Alparegho, Like Nothing Else - Hélène Sanguinetti (French-English/dual-language), trans. Ann Cefola [2019]
High Tide Of The Eyes - Bijan Elahi (Farsi-English/dual-language) trans. Rebecca Ruth Gould and Kayvan Tahmasebian [2019]

An Absence So Great and Spontaneous It Is Evidence of Light - Anne Gorrick [2018]
The Book of Everyday Instruction - Chloe Bass [2018]
Executive Orders Vol. II - a collaboration with the Organism for Poetic Research [2018]
One More Revolution - Andrea Mazzariello [2018]
The Suitcase Tree - Filip Marinovich [2018]
Chlorosis - Michael Flatt and Derrick Mund [2018]
Susurros a Mi Padre - Erick Sáenz [2018]
Sharing Plastic - Blake Nemec [2018]
The Book of Sounds - Mehdi Navid (Farsi dual language, trans. Tina Rahimi) [2018]
In Corpore Sano : Creative Practice and the Challenged Body [Anthology, 2018]; Lynne DeSilva-Johnson and Jay Besemer, co-editors
Abandoners - Lesley Ann Wheeler [2018]
Jazzercise is a Language - Gabriel Ojeda-Sague [2018]
Return Trip / Viaje Al Regreso - Israel Dominguez; (Spanish-English dual language) trans. Margaret Randall [2018]
Born Again - Ivy Johnson [2018]
Attendance - Rocío Carlos and Rachel McLeod Kaminer [2018]
Singing for Nothing - Wally Swist [2018]
The Ways of the Monster - Jay Besemer [2018]
Walking Away From Explosions in Slow Motion - Gregory Crosby [2018]
The Unspoken - Bob Holman [Bowery Books imprint - 2018]
Field Guide to Autobiography - Melissa Eleftherion [2018]
Kawsay: The Flame of the Jungle - María Vázquez Valdez (Spanish-English dual language) trans. Margaret Randall [2018]
CHAPBOOK SERIES 2018 : Greater Grave - Jacq Greyja; Needles of Itching Feathers - Jared Schlickling; Want-Catcher - Adra Raine; We, The Monstrous - Mark DuCharme

Lost City Hydrothermal Field - Peter Milne Greiner [2017]
An Exercise in Necromancy - Patrick Roche [Bowery Poetry Imprint, 2017]
Love, Robot - Margaret Rhee[2017]
La Comandante Maya - Rita Valdivia (dual language, trans. Margaret Randall) [2017]
The Furies - William Considine [2017]
Nothing Is Wasted - Shabnam Piryaei [2017]
Mary of the Seas - Joanna C. Valente [2017]
Secret-Telling Bones - Jessica Tyner Mehta [2017]

CHAPBOOK SERIES 2017 : INCANTATIONS
featuring original cover art by Barbara Byers
sp. - Susan Charkes; Radio Poems - Jeffrey Cyphers Wright; Fixing a Witch/Hexing the Stitch - Jacklyn Janeksela; cosmos a personal voyage by carl sagan ann druyan steven sotor and me - Connie Mae Oliver
Flower World Variations, Expanded Edition/Reissue - Jerome Rothenberg and Harold Cohen [2017]
What the Werewolf Told Them / Lo Que Les Dijo El Licántropo - Chely Lima (Spanish-English dual language) trans. Margaret Randall) [2017]
The Color She Gave Gravity - Stephanie Heit [2017]
The Science of Things Familiar - Johnny Damm [Graphic Hybrid, 2017]
agon - Judith Goldman [2017]
To Have Been There Then / Estar Allí Entonces - Gregory Randall (trans. Margaret Randall) [2017]

Instructions Within - Ashraf Fayadh [2016] Arabic-English dual language edition; Mona Kareem, Mona Zaki, and Jonathan Wright, translators
Let it Die Hungry - Caits Meissner [2016]
A GUN SHOW - Adam Sliwinski and Lynne DeSilva-Johnson; Sō Percussion in Performance with Ain Gordon and Emily Johnson [2016]
Everybody's Automat [2016] - Mark Gurarie
How to Survive the Coming Collapse of Civilization [2016] - Sparrow
CHAPBOOK SERIES 2016: OF SOUND MIND **featuring the quilt drawings of Daphne Taylor:* Improper Maps - Alex Crowley; While Listening - Alaina Ferris; Chords - Peter Longofono; Any Seam or Needlework - Stanford Cheung

TEN FOUR - Poems, Translations, Variations [2015]- Jerome Rothenberg, Ariel Resnikoff, Mikhl Likht
MARILYN [2015] - Amanda Ngoho Reavey
CHAPBOOK SERIES 2015: OF SYSTEMS OF **featuring original cover art by Emma Steinkraus:* Cyclorama - Davy Knittle; The Sensitive Boy Slumber Party Manifesto - Joseph Cuillier; Neptune Court - Anton Yakovlev; Schema - Anurak Saelow
SAY/MIRROR [2015; 2nd edition 2016] - JP HOWARD
Moons Of Jupiter/Tales From The Schminke Tub [plays, 2014] - Steve Danziger

CHAPBOOK SERIES 2014: BY HAND: Pull, A Ballad - Maryam Parhizkar; Can You See that Sound - Jeff Musillo; Executive Producer Chris Carter - Peter Milne Greiner; Spooky Action at a Distance - Gregory Crosby;

CHAPBOOK SERIES 2013: WOODBLOCK
**featuring original prints from Kevin William Reed*
Strange Coherence - Bill Considine; The Sword of Things - Tony Hoffman; Talk About Man Proof - Lancelot Runge / John Kropa; An Admission as a Warning Against the Value of Our Conclusions -Alexis Quinlan

DOC U MENT

/däkyəmənt/

First meant "instruction" or "evidence," whether written or not.

noun - a piece of written, printed, or electronic matter that provides information or evidence or that serves as an official record
verb - record (something) in written, photographic, or other form
synonyms - paper - deed - record - writing - act - instrument

[*Middle English, precept, from Old French, from Latin documentum, example, proof, from docre, to teach; see dek- in Indo-European roots.*]

Who is responsible for the manufacture of value?

Based on what supercilious ontology have we landed in a space where we vie against other creative people in vain pursuit of the fleeting credibilities of the scarcity economy, rather than freely collaborating and sharing openly with each other in ecstatic celebration of MAKING?

While we understand and acknowledge the economic pressures and fear-mongering that threatens to dominate and crush the creative impulse, we also believe that ***now more than ever we have the tools to relinquish agency via cooperative means,*** fueled by the fires of the Open Source Movement.

Looking out across the invisible vistas of that rhizomatic parallel country we can begin to see our community beyond constraints, in the place where intention meets resilient, proactive, collaborative organization.

Here is a document born of that belief, sown purely of imagination and will.
When we document we assert.
We print to make real, to reify our being there.
When we do so with mindful intention to address our process,
to open our work to others, to create beauty in words in space,
to respect and acknowledge the strength of the page we now hold physical,
a thing in our hand… we remind ourselves that, like Dorothy:
we had the power all along, my dears.

THE PRINT! DOCUMENT SERIES

is a project of

the trouble with bartleby

in collaboration with

the operating system

www.ingramcontent.com/pod-product-compliance
Lightning Source LLC
Chambersburg PA
CBHW071750080526
44588CB00013B/2199
* 9 7 8 1 9 4 6 0 3 1 3 7 2 *